Off to School

Poems for the Playground

Compiled by Tony Bradman

Illustrated by Tony Blundell

MACDONALD YOUNG BOOKS

New Term

New term,
New school,
New class,
New rules.

New desk,
New names,
New shoes,
New games.

New coat,
New hooks,
New rooms,
New books.

New bag,
New pens,
New food,
New friends.

Colin West

I went to our school tomorrow

I went to our school tomorrow
I got out a pencil of chalk
  The teacher said, 'No silence.
I want you to talk and talk.'
We had our PE on the ceiling
  And assembly under the floor
    The teachers all wrote backwards
In tests there was no score
  The caretaker dropped mud on the carpet
The secretary typed with her toes
  The gerbils ran round the classroom
    And dived on the teacher's nose
    Grumpy Miss Smythe got friendly
    She even told us a joke
    The goldfish swam through the air
    Doing a neat back-stroke
I ran to the entrance to exit
And got home before I set out
If I go to that school last year
  They'll certainly teach me nowt

Ivan Jones

Off to School . . .

Blue ribbons in my hair,
shoes tightened on my feet,
bag loaded till it's square,
the way Mum likes it, neat.

Pencils, pens in order,
lunch box tucked in place,
swimsuit and recorder . . .
There's not a puff of space.

A towel roly-poly,
money for next week's trip.
Check my bag's not holey
now to close the zip.

Reading book in folder,
my backpack chock-a-block,
humped upon my shoulder,
packed solid as a rock.

And Home Again

Carrying my jacket,
damp towel round my wrist –
couldn't stop to pack it –
my T-shirt in a twist.

Swimsuit trawling gutter
past half an apple core,
I'm weighed down with clutter,
a note from Sir, what's more.

Giant painting in one hand,
school hamster in a box.
Walk? It's hard enough to stand
when loaded like an ox.

Backpack slack, not brimming.
Inside: one screwed-up vest
discovered after swimming
left over when I dressed.

Sylvia Turner

The Late Worm

Mummy says I take too long to dress,
And that I fuss when she combs my hair,
And that I dilly-dally over breakfast,
And that I walk too slow to school.

Today,
The school-keeper
Closed the gate
On the dot
of five to nine,
So once again
Into the Late Book,
My teacher puts my name.
'Try not to be late,' she says,
'And remember,
It's the early bird
That gets the worm.'

'But Miss,' I say,
'The late worm misses the early bird,
And lives to wriggle another day.'

'Don't be too sure about that,' she says,
'For just as there are late worms,
So too there are late birds –
And they are usually the hungriest ones!'

Errol Lloyd

A Slip of the Tongue

That thing I said,
It just came out,
I wasn't thinking.

And all at once
the whole class
burst out laughing.

Our teacher
didn't mind, I'm
sure I'm right.

But my face
went redder than
a traffic light!

Bill Bentley's
grin said,
'You're a dummy!'

That time I went
and called our teacher
– 'Mummy!'

Emily Smith

Confessions of a Runner

On my first day at school
My sister cried and cried
On my first day at school
I could have died and died
On my first day at school
My twin embarrassed me
On my first day at school
I learnt schoolology.

On my second day at school
My sister wouldn't come
On my second day at school
She was dragged there by my Mom
On my second day at school
I came dressed in pink
On my second day at school
I was made to think.

On my third day at school
I explored everywhere
On my third day at school
I fell offa my chair
On my third day at school
We all went for a swim
On my third day at school
I cried just like my twin.

On my fourth day at school
They made me run in shorts
On my fourth day at school
I discovered sports
On my fourth day at school
I ran fast and far
On my fourth day at school
I earnt myself a star.

On my fifth day at school
We had tomato crumble
On my fifth day at school
I began to grumble
On my fifth day at school
My teacher got stuck in red tape
On my fifth day at school
Me and my twin escaped.

Benjamin Zephaniah

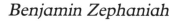

Teacher's Desk

E lastic bands (confiscated)
A box of tissues (one left)
C up of tea (cold)
H anky (for runny noses)
E ggboxes (useful)
R egister
S ausage roll (half chewed)

D iary (last year's)
E lastoplasts (for cut knees)
S ellotape (used up)
K ind words (unlimited supply)

Roger Stevens

The Strangest School Secretary

She's Queen Wasp of the Office,
  her throne's a swivel chair.
Her fingernails are purple.
  A wren nests in her hair.

Her eyes are green as seaweed,
  she has a wildcat's stare.
She growls at timid teachers
  just like a grizzly bear.

To visitors and parents
  she gives an eagle's glare.
Headmaster! Won't you sack her?
  You're right! He'd never dare!

Our secretary's the strangest,
  she's really rather rare.
She's Queen Wasp of the Office,
  her throne's a swivel chair.

Wes Magee

How to Spell ~~yot~~ ~~yatch~~ ~~yotch~~ Yacht

Once I had learnt that c-a-t spelt **cat**,
It wasn't hard to see
That b-a-t was **bat**
And h-a-t and m-a-t
Were **hat** and **mat**.

And when Miss Petty showed me d-o-g
(And that spelt **dog**),
I soon worked out that l-o-g was **log**,
And h-o-g was **hog**,
And f and r and o and g spelt **frog**.

I drew them in my book
So everyone could look,
And wrote the words as well,
To show that I could spell!

And next I learnt that d-o-t spelt **dot**.
I drew a little **bot**
For all to see,
And wrote beside it b-o-t;
And then, I don't know what –
A **spot**, a **cot**, a **chimney pot**.

And THEN
I drew a lovely boat
With windy sails, afloat,
And next to it I wrote
In huge great letters, Y–O–T.
It made me cross to see
That cross, in nice Miss Petty's red ink pen.

I thought it wasn't fair
What I saw there.
How could **yot** be
That silly y-a-c-h-t?

And so I sucked my thumb
And cried – and said I'd tell.
And I went home and told my mum
Miss Petty couldn't spell.

Gerard Benson

Word-Watching

He has drawn lines
Half-way down the page
And covered them
With half a story.

Now he pauses,
Searching the air.

If he draws another line
And keeps very still,
Perhaps some words
Will come and sit on it.

Wendy Cope

nce there was a sm
jalk in the woods an
 a hors. It was a v
d do you wont to c
oy and the boy hoos n
ig teeth and I think
iors. Then the wolf got
st but he wood come back soon and the boy called billy thort he
ood hiy hide. Sudenly he looked and he saw a big pig with a
eet wheelbarrow walking threw the woods.

who went for a wark
he met a wolf riding
ingry wolf and he
a ride on my hors little
 billy sed no you have
eat me if I ride on yor
gry and road off very

quick   run   growl   wolf
boy   hungry   pig   eat
woods   home
teeth

The Dinner-Lady

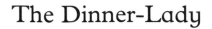

The dinner-lady said to me,
'You're taking far too long.
You finish up that lovely cod:
It makes you big and strong.'

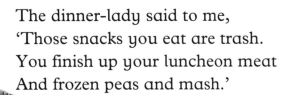

The dinner-lady said to me,
'Those toffee-bars aren't nice.
You finish up your shepherd's pie,
And then your prunes and rice.'

The dinner-lady said to me,
'Those snacks you eat are trash.
You finish up your luncheon meat
And frozen peas and mash.'

But, peering through the serving-hatch
I swear it made me blink,
I saw her with her bag of crisps
And tin of fizzy drink.

John Yeoman

Lunch Box

Lunch boxes,
Munch boxes,
Pink, blue, red!
I've got cheese and apple
and thirteen loaves of bread!

Lunch boxes,
Munch boxes,
Yellow, white, blue!
I've got twenty sandwiches,
How about you?

Lunch boxes,
Munch boxes,
Brown, black, pink!
Mine is full of jelly beans
(At least, that's what I *think!*)

Lunch boxes,
Munch boxes,
Purple, orange, green!
Mine is full of chocolate drops
and strawberry ice-cream!

Lunch boxes,
Munch boxes,
Scarlet, emerald, grey!
Mine's a finger-licking secret . . .
What's in *yours* today?

Judith Nicholls

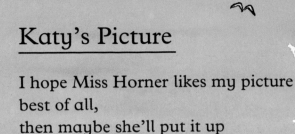

Katy's Picture

I hope Miss Horner likes my picture
best of all,
then maybe she'll put it up
on the classroom wall.

I'll have bright blue at the bottom to be sea
and pale blue at the top to be the sky.
I'll put in waves like frilly bits of lace
(Miss Horner has a blouse with cuffs like that).
I'll put the sun in, with a smiling face
and a grey donkey in a big straw hat.

I'll paint a pirate ship with wide, white sails
puffed up because the wind is blowing gales.

And . . .

I'd like a mermaid combing
her hair with a golden comb
and a lighthouse so that sailors
can find a safe way home.

Adèle Geras

Day Dreamer

Everybody's hand is up.
Except mine.
What's the answer?
What's the question?
I was TRYING to listen
To what she was saying.
But other thoughts
Crept into my head
And my mind went straying.

Don't pick on me
In front of the class.
Don't say
We're waiting!
Did you hear what I asked?
Don't say
Well, thank you for joining us
At last.

Put up my hand
Like the others.
Pretend that I know.
Yes? she says to me,
And I say, *Oh –*
I've forgotten, Miss.

Pat Moon

Science is Magic

We kept a bean seed wet and warm
And in a week or two
A twisty shoot came out of it
And grew, and grew, and GREW.
We had a hamster, called him Bill,
But were amazed to see
One day there were NINE BABIES.
Bill must have been . . . a *she*!

**Teacher says it's Science
And it's magic.**

We fixed a battery on a board;
We wired the circuit right
And joined it at the other end
To buzzer, bell or light.
I rang and rang and rang my bell
Till we began to say:
'That sounded like the lesson bell.'
So we all ran out to play.

**Teacher says it's Science
And it's magic.**

Eileen Round

J Bill
our class
hamster.

Worm Sandwich

A boy in the playground swore
    he'd never tell a lie,
Crossed his heart,
And hoped to die.
He said, 'I had a sandwich
    the other week,
Filled with worms and bubble
    and squeak.
The worms were wriggling
    trying to escape,
So I had to stick it up with Sellotape.'
I looked at him,
His eyes were blue,
Staring, calm and clear and true.
He was lying of course,
But just in case,
I told him I'd had slugs for tea,
Wrapped in nettles,
Baked in a tin,
And fixed together,
With a safety pin.

Rachel Dixon

Ten School Computers

Ten school computers all on line:
one went down and then there were nine.

Nine school computers, until my mate
blew one up, and then there were eight.

Eight school computers, but one was loaned from Devon
and had to be returned, and then there were seven.

Seven school computers, but one always sticks,
so that was no good, and then there were six.

Six school computers, but one belonged to Clive
and he took it home, and then there were five.

Five school computers, but one fell on the floor
and then it wouldn't work, and then there were four.

Four school computers, but one's for class B,
so we couldn't use that one, and then there were three.

Three school computers, till someone spilt some glue
which gummed one up, and then there were two.

Two school computers, but one was left in the sun
and it burst into flames, and then there was one.

One school computer. 'Children, DON'T RUN!'
Bang, crash, tinkle . . . and then there were none!

Charles Thomson

Arithmetic

She takes ten and divides it by three:
it breaks, hard-edged, echoing.

She divides a wet sky by a high window,
she wants to add a radio, take away the teacher.
The day isn't working out right.

She's given up caring about correct answers.
That makes the sums easy. So easy it bores her.

She measures the drawn-out length of the lesson
against the chipped edge of the desk – and still
finds it's too long till the bell.

She counts up her friends and subtracts
her enemies. Now that's interesting

but difficult, difficult.

David Calder

Spot What I've Got

Feeling cold,
feeling hot,
shivery,
quivery . . .
What've I got?

Feeling sick,
feeling weak,
scratching,
itching for a week . . .

pick 'em,
burst 'em,
blobby spots,
crusty scabs
of
chickenpox.

Gina Douthwaite

Plague Around

There's a plague around
There's a plague around
In every village
and every town

With big purple spots
and greenish ones too
There's a plague around
and it's waiting for you

There's a plague around
There's a plague around
Keep your eyes open
and don't make a sound

Or your ears will flap
and you'll start to cough
You'll sneeze and sneeze
till your nose drops off

There's a plague around
There's a plague around
In every school
There's a playground

You'll burst out laughing
and run around
when you get into
The playground

There's a playground
There's a playground
In every school
There's a playground

Roger McGough

Gus the Hamster

Gus is out! Don't move! Don't shout!
Gus the classroom hamster's out!
He's left his cage. He's lost somewhere –
Search high and low, search here and there!
Inside the cupboards, behind each book,
Everywhere we can we look.
But Gus is gone. No sign of him
Until . . .

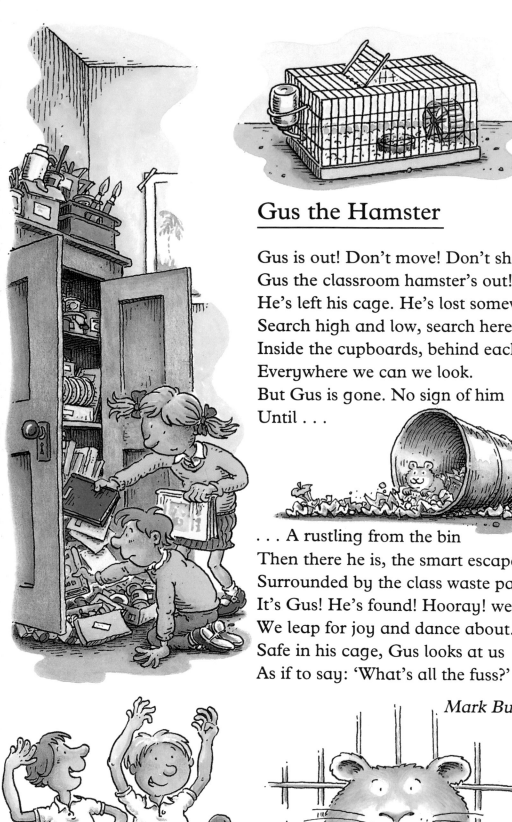

. . . A rustling from the bin
Then there he is, the smart escaper!
Surrounded by the class waste paper.
It's Gus! He's found! Hooray! we shout,
We leap for joy and dance about.
Safe in his cage, Gus looks at us
As if to say: 'What's all the fuss?'

Mark Burgess

The Painted Jungle

There's a lion close behind you
And a tiger near to me.
A lizard creeps across the leaves
And a sloth hangs in a tree.

A spider spins a giant web
As giraffe peeps out up high.
Above the forest two white doves
Sail across the sky.

Butterflies drift between the flowers,
Snake slithers past beneath.
Elephant swings his mighty trunk
As crocodile shows his teeth.

Watch the agile monkeys swing,
Hear the parrots call,
Across the painted jungle
On our playground wall.

A. Holden

Story Time

At the dark end of day.
Our work's put away,
And we all sit there
By the teacher's old chair
For story time.

Teacher reads in a whisper.
We don't say a word.
She reads about ghosts
And a magical bird.
She reads about silver
And jewels and gold.
She reads about witches
Wrinkled and old.
She reads about princes
In bright rainbow coats;
About troublesome trolls
And three trip-trap goats.

She reads about giants
And a weird magic bean,
Describing strange worlds
Which we've never seen.
She reads about poor boys
And princesses proud.
She makes us see camels
Hiding there in a cloud.
She's got hundreds of voices:
Gruff, gentle, shrill, deep.
Some listen with eyes closed,
But none falls asleep.
We all keep so still,
Not one word to say,
As we sit there quite hushed
At the dark end of day.

John Kitching

All the voices have gone

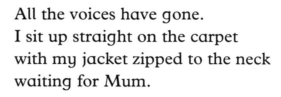

All the voices have gone.
I sit up straight on the carpet
with my jacket zipped to the neck
waiting for Mum.

I hold my lunch box tight
and my bonfire painting.
Miss says, *Right,*
no point sitting there waiting.

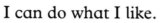

I can do what I like.
I can build roads in the sand,
I can have the red digger all the time
and not take turns.

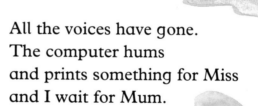

All the voices have gone.
The computer hums
and prints something for Miss
and I wait for Mum.

I sit up straight on the carpet
with my jacket zipped to the neck
while Miss works at her desk
and I watch the door for Mum.

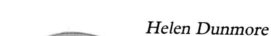

If I shut my eyes then open them
she'll come.

Helen Dunmore

Tony Bradman and Macdonald Young Books would like to thank the following for contributing to this collection:

'New Term' © **Colin West** 1998
'I went to our school tomorrow' © **Ivan Jones** 1998
'Off to School... And Home Again' © **Sylvia Turner** 1998
'The Late Worm' © **Errol Lloyd** 1998
'A Slip of the Tongue' © **Emily Smith** 1998
'Confessions of a Runner' © **Benjamin Zephaniah** 1998
'Teacher's Desk' © **Roger Stevens** 1998
'The Strangest School Secretary' © **Wes Magee** 1998
'How to Spell ~~Yot~~ ~~Yatch~~ ~~Yotch~~ Yacht © **Gerard Benson** 1998
'Word Watching' © **Wendy Cope** 1998
'The Dinner-Lady' © **John Yeoman** 1998
'Lunch Box' from *Higgledy-Humbug* by **Judith Nicholls** published by Mary Glasgow Publications Ltd 1990, reprinted by permission of the author.
'Katy's Picture' © **Adèle Geras** 1998
'Day Dreamer' © **Pat Moon** 1998
'Science is Magic' © **Eileen Round** 1998
'Worm Sandwich' © **Rachel Dixon** 1998
'Ten School Computers' © **Charles Thomson** 1998
'Arithmetic' © **David Calder** 1998
'Spot What I've Got' © **Gina Douthwaite** 1998
'Plague Around' © **Roger McGough** 1998
'Gus the Hamster' © **Mark Burgess** 1998
'The Painted Jungle' © **A. Holden** 1998
'Story Time' © **John Kitching** 1998
'All the voices have gone' © **Helen Dunmore** 1998